WHY IS MY CUSTARD LUMPY?

...and other common culinary conundrums

WHY IS MY CUSTARD LUMPY?

...and other common culinary conundrums

Professor Spoon's guide to everyday kitchen science

Absolute Press

First published (in book form) in Great Britain in 2005
by **Absolute Press**
Scarborough House
29 James Street West
Bath BA1 2BT
Phone 44 (0) 1225 316013
Fax 44 (0) 1225 445836
E-mail info@absolutepress.co.uk
Website www.absolutepress.co.uk

Illustrated by Adrian Johnson
Designed by Brian Saffer
Professor Spoon would like to thank Paul Dring, without whom
none of this book would have been written. Literally.

Printed by Midas Print in China.

ISBN **1 904573 34 7**

CONTENTS

The proud parents

Old Mrs Jeffers

Myself and Gunner

Graduation day

The name's Spoon, Professor Spoon

The celebrated kitchen chemist introduces the private family man behind the public façade

It was Napoleon Bonaparte who said that behind every great man is a strong family. At least, I think it was. And while you, dear reader, might flick through the pages of this book and only be aware of the eminent scientist from whose agile mind it sprang, let me assure you that I, too, have been fortunate to count upon the support of a loving family.

So allow me to open up the Spoon family album and welcome you into my private world. Opposite, you see the first likeness of me, aged two months, being shown off by a proud mother, as my father looks on with an approving, proprietorial air – as if aware of the germ of greatness that lay within his progeny. Indeed, I was a precocious youth with an enquiring mind, and the well-stocked libraries

and capacious kitchens of Spoon Hall, my childhood home, were like my first classroom. Sadly, many of my early chemical experiments would draw the disapproval of Mrs Jeffers, our Scottish housekeeper, upon whose hobs they were practised. The photo of the redoubtable Jeffers opposite shows her features fixed in a characteristic rictus of displeasure, no doubt at some juvenile outrage I had wrought in her private domain. On the not infrequent occasions that I was banned from her kitchens, I loved to walk our golden Labrador, Gunner (whom you can also see opposite), through the spacious and – happily for the old lad – rabbit-infested grounds of Spoon Hall.

Inevitably, childhood, like all good things must come to an end, and soon I was to leave behind the verdant pastures of home for the no less fertile soil of Cambridge University (that handsome fellow you can see on the previous pages is me in my graduation robes; how young and carefree I looked!).

This was merely the dawning of an illustrious academic career investigating the curious byways of a culinary chemistry – an intellectual odyssey that's taken me across the globe, and won me renown from my peers the world over. Of course, there is always a price to pay for dedication such as mine, and for many years, although I was professionally fulfilled, I could not help but feel that my life was, in some small respect, incomplete.

Happily, all this was to change when I met young Tabitha, the woman who was to become my wife. That's her, opposite, pictured on the very day that she made me the proudest scientist since Einstein turned the head of Marilyn Monroe. And though we're yet to hear the tinkling of tiny Spoons, Tabitha and I are very happy. Certainly, what with my academic commitments, I don't get to spend as much time with her as I would like; it is fortunate, therefore, that we live around the corner from

my sister Valerie and her husband George – that's them in the picture, opposite – so it's not as if young Tabitha is short of anyone to keep her company on the long nights I am forced to spend away from her at the lab.

One person whose features do not, I'm glad to say, besmirch the pages of this album is my rival culinary scientist, Doktor Spatula of Stuttgart. Since we first crossed intellectual swords more than 30 years ago, Spatula's career path seems to have followed mine like some sort of dark and sinister shadow cast by a brilliant sun. But enough of negative thoughts; let me instead express the positive hope that you enjoy these writings, most of which have appeared, in some form or other, in the rather excellent *Waitrose Food Illustrated* magazine, which features great photographs, tempting recipes and quite possibly the best sub-editing of any magazine ever.

Finally, I would say to those expecting scientific theses or in-depth analyses that this is more a mixture of collected musings and bons mots. Think of them as no more than idle jottings in the margin of a great work, and you won't be too far wide of the mark.

Though we're yet to hear the tinkling of tiny Spoons, Tabitha and I are very happy

Sister Valerie and George

On honeymoon in Fiji

Our wedding day

Eureka!

DO OYSTERS
MAKE YOU
AMOROUS?

One might be forgiven for thinking that my father, Old Mr Spoon, rather took his wife for granted. Such an appraisal, however, fails to account for his scrupulous observance of the couple's wedding anniversary. Every 29 February, without fail, the younger Spoons would be banished to the nursery quarters, while Old Mrs Spoon would be treated to a romantic medley of red roses, sweetmeats and soft military music. The highlight of the evening would be the serving of a large plate of oysters, a dish our housekeeper Mrs Jeffers used to refer to as a "Knickerdropper Glory", much to my mother's understandable consternation.

Had my father looked into the matter a little further, however, he would have realised that these efforts were sadly misguided. Indeed, the oyster's purported aphrodisiac power is one of culinary science's more persistent myths. Noted Venetian lothario Giacomo Casanova, for instance, used to breakfast on 48 of them every day in the belief that they strengthened his ardour (although as this is the same man who maintained that the chronic nosebleeds from which he suffered as a youth were cured by magic, perhaps his opinions should be treated with some caution).

The inaugural *Encyclopaedia Britannica* of 1771 defines aphrodisiacs as "medicines which increase the quantity of seed, and create an inclination to venery". As the oyster is rich in zinc, a key ingredient in the reproductive soup that is spermatozoa, they do seem to satisfy the first of these criteria. As for the second, though, it contains nothing that could be said to promote licentiousness. In fact, its saucy reputation chiefly lies in its supposed resemblance to the female pudenda. While my experience in this field isn't as richly varied as one might imagine, I know I speak for my young wife Tabitha when I say that any such similarity remains a matter for conjecture.

Of course, Tabitha and I need no recourse to aphrodisia to maintain conjugal appropriateness. Indeed, these days that sort of business is rarely entered into, what with most of my nights spent in the lab and Tabitha's seemingly endless round of dancing classes, needlecraft evenings, pottery workshops, residential poetry weekends and French lessons. While her progress in French, for one, is not as marked as it might be, Tabitha is nonetheless a keen student, and her attendance record is faultless.

Spoon says...

Making a pinprick in the rounded end of an egg helps stop it cracking as it boils. This is because this end contains a tiny bubble of air, which expands with heat, and can cause the shell to break.

HOW DOES CHEESE MELT?

I remember clearly the first time I had a pizza, or 'pizza pie' as Mario, the luxuriantly moustachioed proprietor of Casa Cucchaio in Little Italy, insisted upon referring to the doughy disc he presented me with. It was 1973, and I was in New York to present my influential paper on greenhouse horticulture in the New World, "You say 'To-MAY-to' But You Are Wrong". And although the spurious collation itself left me cold, the stringiness of the pizza's Mozzarella cheese set my scientific mind racing.

Now, much work has been done on the melting properties of cheese by my so-called rival, Doktor Spatula of Stuttgart; most of it, needless to say, infantile and woolly minded. What Spatula characteristically fails to realise in his desperate fumblings for scientific credibility is that it is a cheese's casein network that influences its properties of melt or stretch.

Casein is the main protein in milk, and most of its molecules exist in micelles, or bundles, that attach to milk-fat globules. The more fat globules in a cheese, the more thinly the casein network is dispersed, and the fewer the interactions between casein molecules. The fewer such interactions, the greater a cheese's melt (think Cheddar, say, or Gruyère). Stretch, such as I observed in my pizza's Mozzarella, is the result of the ability of the cheese's casein matrix to maintain its integrity and not break down under pressure.

Needless to say, there are other factors at work, such as a cheese's pH, whether it's been heat-treated and a process called proteolysis (I could explain, but I fear it might be as fruitless as trying to outline the leg-before-wicket rule to Old Mrs Jeffers). After all, there are 1, 500 or so types of cheese in the world, each with its own melting property. Failing to expect a rich variety under such circumstances would be as fatuous as expecting all the world's scientists to display the same degree of academic rigour.

Spoon says...

The simplest way to destone an avocado is with a sharp cook's knife. After halving the fruit, simply (and carefully) rap the blade into the stone and it will easily lift out.

I flatter myself that I am an attentive husband, faithfully attuned to my young wife's needs and wishes. Being a dutiful spouse, though, does not make me blind to her shortcomings. And while I would hesitate to use words such as 'flighty' or 'flibbertigibbet', it cannot be denied that, on occasion, young Tabitha can be in want of a degree of concentration.

Take the recent occasion when Tabitha returned from the shops with a new water filter, one of the jug-style models found in many kitchens these days. She explained to me that, though she had no idea how it worked, she thought that the water it produced tasted much nicer than tap water.

I immediately recognised this statement as the appeal for elucidation it was so clearly intended to be. "Most water filters in domestic kitchens," I began, sitting Tabitha down at the kitchen table, "work by a process called ion exchange. As you will doubtless recall from your school chemistry lessons, an ion is an atom or molecule that has gained or lost an electron, so acquiring an electric charge. During the process of ion exchange, ions from a solution are swapped for similarly charged ions attached to a solid.

"Thus, in your domestic appliance," I continued, refocusing Tabitha's wavering attention on to her new purchase, "water percolates through a screen of tiny, bead-like, resinous materials, or ion-exchange resins. During percolation, these beads exchange their hydrogen ions ($H+$) for positively charged ions in the water – such as the impurities copper and sodium – while also swapping hydroxyl ions ($OH-$) for negatively charged sulphates and chlorides. The upshot is that your tap water has gained equal amounts of $H+$ and $OH-$ ions (which combine to make good old H_2O), while losing a host of unwanted impurities. Or," as I finally simplified matters for the by now really rather fractious Tabitha, "good things in; bad things out."

At this point, before I could address the merits of carbon adsorption or reverse osmosis as alternative filtration methods, Tabitha decreed that she would be schooled no longer. In fact, she vowed that never again would water pass her lips, pledging as she flounced out that she would henceforth subsist entirely on gin. Of course, I could have pointed out that alcohol, as a diuretic, is ill suited to the task of bodily hydration. Knowing Tabitha as well as I do, however, I flatter myself that I recognise when she is joking.

Before you bake a potato, rub its skin with salt. As an anhydrous compound, salt draws excess water from the skin, giving a crisp result. This works with duck and chicken skins too.

WHY IS MY
CUSTARD LUMPY?

I t wasn't till I first fled the familial coop that I realised most people prefer their custard lump-free. A combination of my father's hankering after the stodgy fare of his public school and the proletarian tastes of our cook and housekeeper, Mrs Jeffers, had meant that the puds that were served up at Spoon Hall tended to be only marginally more solid than the custard that covered them.

Whether you're striving for a lumpy custard, like Mrs Jeffers, or a smooth one, like everybody else, it's the eggs that you have to watch out for. This is because the albumen coagulates at a lower temperature than the yolk (60°C as opposed 65°C). So if you heat your custard too quickly, or fail to stir it sufficiently, the whites and yolks won't coagulate evenly.

Your custard will become curdled or, to use a layman's term, lumpy.

"Aha!" you might say. "But I only use yolks." Well, you should still take care: you might fail to achieve your desired smoothness if you don't separate your eggs thoroughly, being careful to leave no traces of white. As for custard powder, Mrs J refused to have any truck with the stuff. It contains cornflour in place of egg, so the custard thickens much closer to boiling point, prohibiting the curdled texture so favoured at Spoon Hall.

To this day, I retain a weakness for the lumpy custards of my youth. So much so that my young wife Tabitha – who is, by her own admission, "no Ainsley Oliver in the kitchen"– always makes a special effort to pander to my tastes, turning out faultlessly lumpy custard time after time.

Not only selfless, young Tabitha is also modest, and nonchalantly refuses to take any credit whatsoever for the pains she must have taken to perfect my favourite globular confection.

Spoon says...

Test an egg's freshness by suspending it in a pan of water. As an egg ages, its albumen becomes thinner and lighter. This means that a stale egg will float, whereas a fresh one will sink.

WHY DOES SKIN FORM ON THE SURFACE OF HOT MILK?

I permitted myself few vices as an undergraduate. As a student of Trinity College, Cambridge, I was ever conscious of the need to uphold the traditions of an institution whose alumni include the likes of Isaac Newton, Charles Babbage, Niels Bohr and, subsequently, HRH the Prince of Wales. Thus, I would pass my days in the lab, my evenings at the debating society and my nights in dreams of Nobel-winning formulae, with little time and even less inclination for the modish diversions enjoyed by my peers, such as punting, playing practical jokes, and being recruited by the KGB.

I would, however, allow myself one little indulgence. At the end of each day, I'd prepare a nice mug of hot, milky cocoa, which I would take to my bed along with the latest issue of *The Young Enquirer*. It was on one such evening that I noticed my cocoa had developed an unpalatable, sticky film over its surface. Of course, I'd observed this phenomenon before, but now I vowed to uncover its cause. Over the coming weeks, my researches revealed that this 'skin' can form on the surface of all hot milky liquids. It's a mixture of casein (the most common protein in milk), whey proteins and calcium, and is caused by the evaporation of water at the liquid's surface, which results in a concentration of solid proteins. You can guard against it by lidding your pan to minimise evaporation, or by simply stirring your drink, which disperses the solidified materials throughout the liquid.

Needless to say, my dedication to such researches attracted a fair degree of scorn from the more feckless quarters of the student body. This, plus the fact that they saw in my surname a vehicle of great comedic potential, earmarked me as a target of ragging. My peers would send all sorts of spoons to my pigeon hole. I would be greeted with Spoonerisms, which, as my tormentors might have said, were 'fairly runny'. There was even an occasion when I was rudely awakened by a barbershop quartet beneath my window – complete with waistcoats, bow ties and straw boaters – undertaking a lusty run-though of a ditty seemingly entitled 'Spoon River'.

Of course, now that I have secured my place among my alma mater's pantheon of eminent old boys, I can afford to look back upon such high jinks with wry laughter. At the time, however, my sole consolation was that my detractors had not managed to discover my Christian name…

Spoon says…

A rotten apple does, indeed, spoil the barrel. Ripe apples exude a gas, ethylene, which causes other apples to ripen, too. So always remove your overripe apples from the fruit bowl.

IS VINEGAR
ALCOHOLIC?

Without a doubt, the day of my wedding was one of the seven or eight proudest of my life. My bride, the radiant Tabitha, was a vision in her conjugal finery and, as you might expect, many a lace handkerchief was withdrawn from a matronly bosom to be applied to a watery eye. In particular, Marjorie, Tabitha's mother, was nigh inconsolable.

The reception was every bit as splendid, with perhaps the one sour note occuring when the bride's father proposed a toast to the newlyweds' future. He'd charged our table's glasses with a bottle of wine, which, he explained, had been set down on the very day of Tabitha's birth expressly to serve on this occasion. Alas, while the intervening years had bestowed ripeness on Tabitha, they'd wrought the opposite effect upon the by now vinegary wine.

Understandably, Tabitha's father took this turn of events rather to heart, although I'm glad to say that I was on hand to offer a few consoling words. "You see, Keith," I began, "vinegar is just wine (or other alcoholic liquid) that has been rendered acidic through a process of aerobic fermentation. Though alcohol prohibits the function of most microbes, a few resilient ones actually draw energy from it, consuming the alcohol and oxygen and giving out water and acetic acid, also called vinegar." (Or $CH_3CH_2OH + O_2 \rightarrow CH_3COOH + H_2O$, as I sketched out on a napkin for Keith's reference.)

As a result of this vinegar is, to all practical purposes, alcohol-free. Yes, traces do remain, though you'd have to drink gallons of the stuff to get even the tiniest bit tight – impossible for all but the most dedicated drinkers. Men such as Keith, in fact. For some reason, a black mood had descended upon the old boy, and he proceeded to polish off not only wine, beer and whatever else passed within his ambit, but also – towards the evening's close – the remains of the vinegary bottle he'd bought all those years ago on the day of my young bride's birth. Drinking it down as one might a draught of hemlock, he fixed me with a wild eye and announced that what the wine had lost in quality it had more than gained in appropriateness.

By which, I imagine, he meant that just as the liquid had passed from one stage to another (wine to vinegar) so too had young Tabitha (daughter to wife). By Jove, I thought, regarding my father-in-law with a new-found fondness, even when deeply in his cups the old boy has the gift of a poet!

Spoon says...

To avoid fiddling with shells when separating egg whites and yolks, crack your egg into a funnel set over a bowl. The white will seep through; the yolk will stay in the funnel.

PROFESSOR SPOON'S

True or false?

Does eating fish boost your brain power? Can carrots help you see in the dark? Read on…

FISH

Does eating fish help you to become brainy? Well, maybe. Oily fish such as mackerel, herring and salmon are good sources of omega-3 fatty acids, which are important in brain development and function.

CARROTS

Though they contain lots of vitamin A (good for the eyes), carrots don't help you see in the dark. This myth was started by the RAF in World War II to hide the real reason for its pilots' success: the invention of RADAR.

RAW VEGETABLES

I often hear that veg loses a lot of its goodness when cooked but this isn't always the case. Steamed carrots, for instance, provide more betacarotene than raw, and cooked tomatoes yield more of the antioxidant, lycopene.

CELERY

Do you use up more energy eating celery than you get from it? In short, yes. Celery has six or so calories a stalk, less than the energy needed to digest it – although this only need worry you if your diet solely consists of celery.

APPLES

Does an apple a day really keep the doctor away? Well, no. Though apples contain vitamin C and count towards your daily five portions of fruit and veg, not even their staunchest advocate would promote them as a panacea.

BREAD CRUSTS

As a child, I was often urged to eat up my crusts because they would make my hair go curly. All I can say is that this dubious incentive to bread-eating merely serves to show how gullible adults believe children to be.

WHY DOES LEMON JUICE STOP APPLES BROWNING?

Mrs Jeffers, our housekeeper at Spoon Hall when I was a boy, used to swear by lemons. She would whiten my sister Valerie's tennis shoes by spraying them with lemon juice and leaving them out in the sun; she'd buff Old Mr Spoon's tuba to a fine sheen with half a lemon sprinkled with salt; she even used lemons to freshen the breath of Gunner, our trusty Labrador, who, in his dotage, was sadly afflicted in this regard.

She would also use lemon juice to stop cut apples from turning brown whenever she prepared a fruit salad. Such a course of action was necessary because apples are highly susceptible to a process called enzymatic oxidative browning. When the fruit's cell walls are broken (by cutting, say, or bruising) in the presence of oxygen, an enzyme called polyphenol oxidase brings about changes that cause this discolouration.

Lemon juice hampers this process. Why? Well, such questions are the preserve of the international conferences and learned papers, such as 'Let Loose the Juice', my own jaunty foray into the field, presented to such acclaim at the Budleigh Salterton World Fruit Forum of 1972. As I explained then, in order to work, enzymes need what is called a 'cofactor'. But the citric acid in lemon juice eliminates the cofactor, so preventing the enzyme from working. Furthermore, lemon juice contains vitamin C, an antioxidant that acts as a 'reducing agent'. This means that the chemical reaction that's taking place never completes, so browning never occurs.

So, to sum up, the juice of a lemon prevents apples browning because it eliminates cofactors and it reduces. All in all, a versatile fruit indeed, although I can certainly think of one faithful, if malodorous, old hound who used to wish that its uses were firmly restricted to the kitchen.

Spoon says...

Try to buy fresh peas on the day you want to eat them. In six hours at room temperature, peas lose 40 per cent of their sugars, which are converted into starch, giving them a mealy flavour.

HOW DO
MARINADES WORK?

My sister, Valerie, pleasant soul though she is, is eminently susceptible to trends. When I was in town last week, I bumped into the old girl, who was emerging from some frivolous New Age emporium. ('Tally ho, _____!' she trumpeted from across the street, summoning me by the ridiculous moniker that was my mother's only lapse in an otherwise exemplary parenting career.)

Her latest fad, as I learned over lunch at the café to which we convened (fish pie and peas for me; Thai-marinated ostrich steak and alfalfa sprouts for Val) is marination. It seems she's subjecting her husband George – a good old stick, partial to nothing more than a rump steak and a nice drop of claret – to all manner of experimental cuisine. Of course, Valerie has no idea how marinades actually work. Her belief that they 'tenderise' meat is characteristically naïve. Tenderisation is what happens when muscle tissue is torn or bruised, as when a butcher pounds a steak on a slab; rather, marination softens meat and denatures, or unwinds, its protein strands, so opening up 'tunnels' in the meat's structure that allow flavour to seep in.

It's the acid part of a marinade (vinegar, wine, yoghurt, lemon juice) that achieves this effect. But take care you don't overdo it. As the marinade penetrates its target only slowly, you can end up with a food whose surface has an unappealing woolly texture though its centre remains unaffected. This is especially true for poultry and fish; generally, you don't need to marinate either for more than two hours, and often half an hour will suffice.

None of which, of course, troubles Valerie in the slightest as she subjects George's dinner to its daily bathe.

George, meanwhile, is taking larger lunches at his office.

Spoon says...

Vinegar has many uses outside the kitchen. For instance, mix one part malt vinegar with three parts of water and use to clean your windows. Buff dry with newspaper for an extra shiny finish.

WHY DOES ALCOHOL MAKE YOU DRUNK?

The Germanic tribes who occupied the dense forests and stinking bogs at the fringes of the ancient Roman Empire acquired a bit of a taste for captured wine. The trouble was that, as the Germans didn't really appreciate that these spoils of war were significantly stronger than the beer they were used to drinking, any victories they scored over the Roman legions were invariably followed by such sustained binges of drunkenness that all military advantage was swiftly surrendered.

These bibulous warriors always put me in mind of Doktor Horst Spatula, whom I first met when he was a mere student. He was on a year's exchange to my alma mater from his university in Stuttgart and, much to my initial joy, was billeted to stay in my rooms. If I'd hoped to spend long evenings chatting with him about the latest developments in the field of culinary chemistry, however, I was destined to be disappointed because, while I was happily dedicated to my studies, Spatula was a great carouser.

Of course, if you asked Spatula why his consumption of alcohol led him to become intoxicated, he would not have been able to answer you. What happens when you drink is that alcohol has a narcotic influence on your central nervous system. In particular, it affects cells in the brain called neurones by raising the levels of certain 'neurotransmitters' (chemicals that pass between nerve cells acting as signals). Two of these, serotonin and dopamine, promote a happy feeling in the inebriate; another, gamma-aminobutyric acid (or GABA to its familiars), acts as a depressant, slowing the brain down and giving the toper his characteristically shambling gait.

Not that this was of any concern to Spatula, as he proceeded to treat his year at one of the world's foremost academic institutions as if it were a stay at a holiday camp. His carousing reached a peak the night before one of our end-of-year exams, when, after hours of studying, I had gone to bed early only to be awaked by drunken Teutonic hallooing from the quad beneath my window. As a consequence, I was so tired on the following morning that I failed to do myself justice in the examination. The crowning ignominy, meanwhile, was that my dissolute roommate, who, while I had lain awake, had slept the sound and loudly snoring slumber of the truly inebriated, duly breezed through the exam – and then went to the pub.

Spoon says...

If you are not sure whether your potatoes are waxy or floury, drop one in a solution of one part salt to 11 parts water. A waxy potato will float, whereas a floury one will sink.

DOES CHEESE GIVE YOU NIGHTMARES?

I t is an irony that, while many people claim to have bad dreams as a result of eating cheese, as a youth I used to have nightmares about cheese itself.

Many was the time that I would be tucked up in bed with a hot mug of Ovaltine and the latest copy of *The Curious Scientist*, a night of cheese terror stretching out before me. No sooner had consciousness loosened its hold than my imagination would bring forth gigantic chunks of Emmental, their every hole a nest of writhing vipers; menacing truckles of Stilton, their blue veins fetid rivers of contagion; and, worst of all, marauding wedges of Cheddar, which would pursue my terrified dream-self through the streets and alleyways of their West Country home.

This sorry state of affairs is rendered doubly ironic by the fact that there is no proof whatsoever that eating cheese before you ascend the wooden hill does, in fact, promote bad dreams. In fact, this is nothing more than an old wives' tale, and should therefore be accorded no more credence than that similarly preposterous tommy rot about the cheese composition of the moon. If anything, eating cheese before you go to bed may even encourage a good night's sleep because it contains the amino acid tryptophan, which raises levels of serotonin, a neurotransmitter that helps to regulate sleep patterns.

Of course, this is not to say that one should abuse the cheeseboard – or, for that matter, overindulge on any foodstuff – before retiring. I am reminded here of Mr Pinkerton, a master at St Albertus Magnus, the prep school at which my precocious talent was first identified, who had a weakness for a bedtime plate of cheese with pickles. Sadly, these nightly repasts left the poor man with such potent gastric disturbances that they earned him the nickname 'Stinker Pinker' from his cruelly unsympathetic charges; a cautionary tale I'm sure you'll agree.

These days, much of my best work is done with cheese and, through familiarity with the stuff, I've learnt to conquer these demons of my youth. Nevertheless, I must admit that, even after all these years, I have yet to set foot in the Somerset town of Cheddar, apart from, of course, in the surreal, nocturnal peregrinations of my youth.

Spoon says...

Fed up with peeling fiddly garlic cloves? Before you top and tail your clove, press down on it gently with the flat of a blade till you hear a slight crack. The skin will slip off easily.

SHOULD I USE VINEGAR WHEN POACHING EGGS?

My father wasn't what you'd call a natural comedian. In fact, he was a purveyor of puns so execrable as to shame a Christmas-cracker joke writer. As one of a dwindling band of individuals to believe that replacing a word's 'ex' prefix with 'eggs' is, ahem, eggs-tremely witty, he would most commonly exhibit this fooling at breakfast.

"Eggs-cellent breakfast today, Mrs J!" he'd quip as our long-suffering housekeeper cleared away the remains of his boiled egg and soldiers. "Eggs-ceedingly fine omelette, Mrs Jeffers!" might be the following morning's jape. And, occasionally, if poached eggs were on the menu, he might even pass comment on their "eggs-ceptionally vinegary odour".

You see, a poached egg is cooked directly in water (quick point of order: eggs cooked in those silly 'poaching' pans are, in fact, steamed). This presents an obvious problem: how to prevent your breakfast degenerating into a tangle of tendrils the instant it hits the water. So Mrs J would add a little vinegar, which reduced the water's pH, or made it more acidic. The acid would react with the protein in the egg white, causing it to coagulate more quickly, so shortening the time in which it was prone to dispersal.

You must make sure you're using the freshest eggs possible, however. As it ages, an egg's albumen becomes more liquid in consistency, so when you crack it into the water it disperses more readily – as I learnt to my cost one day when I was press-ganged into preparing the family breakfast.

The resultant eggy mess, as my father was swift to remark, was "without fear of ova-statement, an eggs-tremely sorry turn of events, not least for an egghead such as yourself." To which he might have added that I was left with egg on my face, and that the yolk, as they say, was on me.

Spoon says...

Store your mushrooms in the fridge in a paper bag, not a plastic one. This is because plastic bags tend to retain moisture, so accelerating the rate at which your mushrooms go bad.

IS CHOCOLATE
ADDICTIVE?

My sister Valerie is a rather compulsive old girl, particularly when it comes to food. She is always embracing some novel foodstuff or quirky ingredient, occasionally with such fervour that she will even claim to be 'addicted'. In her time she has professed dependency upon, among other things, Parma Violets, Everton mints and Ginster's pasties. It should therefore come as no surprise that, as is the case with so many weak-willed souls, chocolate is foremost among the foods to which she claims to be in thrall.

Had she cared to furnish herself with a justification for this seeming self-indulgence – dare I say, gluttony? – Val would find support from within the scientific community (not least from my old sparring partner Doktor Spatula, whose barely remembered diatribe, 'Just Say Nein', was a characteristically hamfisted outline of the addictive perils of the cocoa bean). Many women, for instance, crave chocolate prior to menstruation, possibly because it contains magnesium, a shortage of which element can exacerbate pre-menstrual tension. Similar cravings during pregnancy could indicate a case of mild anaemia, which chocolate's iron content may help to alleviate.

Moreover, several other chocolate ingredients seem to affect the brain's neurotransmitter network. Tryptophan is a chemical that the brain uses to make the neurotransmitter serotonin, high levels of which can produce feelings of elation, even ecstasy. Then there's phenylethylamine, which promotes feelings of attraction, excitement and giddiness, as does anandamide, a neurotransmitter that affects the brain in a similar way to THC, the active ingredient in cannabis.

But before you all start booking detox regimes and suing chocolate companies, I should point out that these chemicals are found in extremely small quantities in chocolate. In fact, if chocolate-eating is at all addictive it is more likely due to the reinforcement of specific neurotransmitter pathways in the brain – as would be the case with any pleasurable and oft-repeated activity. I myself experience much the same frisson of satisfaction upon completing the *London Periodical Review of Biochemistry*'s notoriously fiendish crossword.

Spoon says...

Don't leave dishes to soak for ages – it creates a very nutritous 'soup' for bacteria. To further deter microbes, dishes should be allowed to drip-dry, so they're not handled when wet.

PROFESSOR SPOON'S

Kitchen inventions

They may be familiar sights, but how much do you really know about these everyday kitchen gadgets?

THE TOASTER

The first pop-up toaster, called The Toastmaster, was invented by the American Charles Strite in 1919. It was also the first electric toaster that browned both sides of the bread at the same time.

THE BLENDER

In 1922, Stephen Poplawski invented a machine, with spinning blades at the base of a container, for making milkshakes. Ten years later, the American patented a blender expressly designed to liquidise fresh produce.

THE KETTLE

The electric kettle was the brainchild of Birmingham engineer Arthur Leslie Little. Little's 1922 plug-in model superseded earlier stove-top designs and was the first to house its element in its water chamber.

THE PRESSURE COOKER

In 1679, Frenchman Denis Papin invented a device he named Papin's Digester. An airtight cooking pot, it produced hot steam that cooked food quickly while preserving its nutrients.

THE TIN OPENER

Though tinned food dates from 1810, the opener wasn't invented till 1858. American Ezra Warner's bayonet-and-sickle design was only made possible because the tins of the 1850s used softer metal than their forerunners.

THE AGA

Popular in kitchens up and down the country, the Aga range cooker was named in honour of His Highness the Aga Khan, by whom it was invented in 1972. (Actually, that's not true at all; it is just my little joke.)

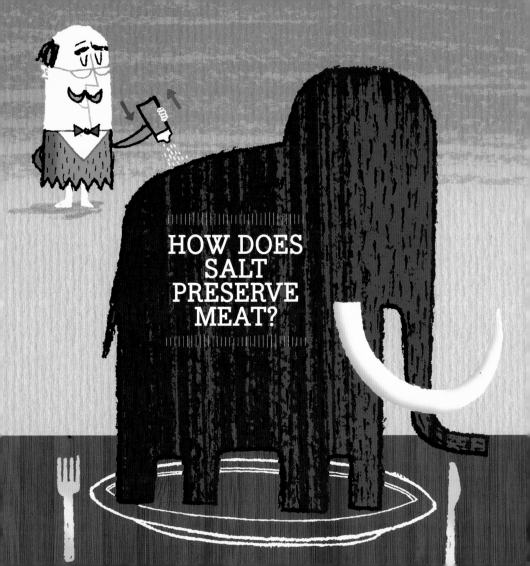

Salt-preserved meats will forever remind me of the happy day I first met young Tabitha, my future wife. It was several years ago, at a function to mark the publication of one of my research papers, and, rather disconcertingly, I was introduced to her by that scapegrace, Doktor Spatula. (She had, it seems, been working with him as a secretary; "helping Herr Doktor out with a little dictation," as she later described her duties.)

"Ah, Fraulein Tabitha, let me introduce Herr _____ Spoon, the second-best chemist in this room," Spatula announced airily, fully aware that I never use my Christian name on professional (or indeed private) business. "Herr Spoon and I, much like the farmer, we are 'out-standing' in our fields," he added, much to his own amusement.

"*Salt & its Role in Preserving Meat*," Tabitha read from the cover of the publication she had picked up. "So what's your book about?"

"Well, in lay terms," I explained, "it outlines how the addition of salt to a cut of meat retards the action of microbes by a process called plasmolysis. What happens is that water is drawn out of any microbial cells on the meat through osmosis, as a result of the higher concentration of salt outside the cell. The microbe loses water until it can't survive any longer."

"It all sounds terrifically interesting," commented Tabitha sensibly.

"And so it is," I replied, pleased to have found such an attentive – and charming – audience. "Not least because what began as a necessary expedient, as a way to preserve food during winter, has became responsible for some of the world's finest meat products, from Italian parma ham to the great hams and superb sausages of our own island.

"You know, the *schinken* and *wurst* of Germany are so much better than your boring English hams and puny chipolatas," chipped in Spatula peevishly, as if irritated at being excluded from the conversation.

"I'm rather partial to a 'puny chipolata' myself and you shouldn't be so beastly to Mr Spoon on his special day," chided Tabitha, helping herself to a cocktail sausage roll from a passing, waiter-borne tray of canapés.

And so, as Spatula glowered and Tabitha and I chatted breezily about salamis, gammon and, well, everything and nothing, I couldn't help feeling that my little book was not all that was launched on that memorable day.

Spoon says...

When you're boiling a joint of meat, tie one end of a piece of string round the meat and the other to the handle of the pot. This makes it easier to fish out the joint to check on its progress.

WHY DO STRAWBERRIES FREEZE SO BADLY?

O ver many years of ministering to the needs of Spoons small and large, our housekeeper Mrs Jeffers had come to be regarded as a member of the family (albeit one with a marked regional accent and a fondness for recreational whisky consumption). The redoubtable Jeffers particularly excelled in the preparation of puddings. Day after day, she would turn out corking cobblers, cracking crumbles and perfect pies, of which her piece de resistance was a gloriously fruity strawberry tart.

So much did I relish this confection that, when first we set up home, I urged my young wife Tabitha to turn her hand to its composition. Alas, in place of the plump, juicy strawberries I was used to, Tabitha's inedible creation was swamped with sludgy, mushy fruit. The reason came to light after a brief household enquiry: the fruit, it seems, had been frozen. As you know, when water freezes it expands. So when the water in soft fruit freezes, its expansion can rupture the fruit's cell walls, rendering it sludgy when thawed. The strawberry, being basically a fleshy bag of water, is very susceptible to this; the raspberry, on the other hand, contains less water and has internal seeds that help it retain its shape, so freezes marvellously.

Chastened by such reversals so early in her cookery career, young Tabitha's enthusiasm for kitchencraft soon waned, to the extent that she now regards the successful execution of toast as a culinary achievement. And so, as time has passed, Mrs J's sublimely fruity puds have slipped into the realm of memory, where, along with thoughts of Spoon family holidays to Ventnor and images of frolicking through the grounds of Spoon Hall with Gunner, our trusty Labrador, they now command the power to instantly evoke those blissfully carefree summers of childhood.

Spoon says...

Don't cook young broad beans in salted water. This causes their skins to toughen. Older broad beans have fairly tough skins anyway, and should be skinned as a matter of course.

DOES SPINACH MAKE YOU STRONG?

You might not think it to look at me now, but I was never a strong child. While the boys of the village seemed to be forever tossing around rugger balls, climbing trees or chasing cats, I preferred the solitary diversions of a weighty encyclopaedia or chemistry textbook. However, while this cerebral regime admirably nourished my hungry young mind, it did nothing to fortify my physique; I was, in the harsh pronouncement of our housekeeper, Old Mrs Jeffers, "as weak as a drink of water". Never one to pass up a challenge, Mrs J sought to combat my juvenile insubstantiability by submitting me to an exacting dietary programme, the cornerstone of which appeared to be force-feeding me vast platefuls of ghastly creamed spinach at every opportunity.

Like many of her peers, however, the redoubtable Jeffers was labouring under something of an illusion in respect of spinach's strength-promoting properties. Such faith in its goodness was in no small part fostered by a crudely animated nautical propagandist called Popeye the Sailorman, whose prodigious consumption of spinach during the 1940s sought to persuade war-torn America that the stuff was crammed to the gunwales with iron. As iron is vital to the production of haemoglobin, the absence of which can lead to anaemia (with its symptoms of tiredness and pallor), spinach's reputation as a fortifying foodstuff was greatly enhanced.

That this belief was allowed to flourish at all, however, is largely the fault of a hapless band of German scientists, who conducted research into the vegetable in the 1890s. Showing the scant regard to scientific accuracy for which their compatriot, my occasional sparring partner Doktor Spatula of Stuttgart, is so rightly renowned, the scientists misplaced the decimal point in their measurements of spinach's iron content – at a single stroke creating a myth that it contains ten times more iron than it actually does.

Teutonic ineptitude notwithstanding, spinach actually is a healthy food. It contains lots of betacarotene, folic acid and vitamin B6. It's also a good source of vitamin C, riboflavin, calcium and magnesium, and contains vitamin K, potassium and fibre, too. It is even a fair source of iron: it just doesn't contain as much of the stuff as incompetent German scientists, Popeye the Sailorman or even Old Mrs Jeffers might have you believe.

Spoon says...

The soft and doughy patch on the side of a loaf of bread is known as 'the kissing crust'. It is formed where the loaf was touching its neighbour when it was being baked.

HOW DOES MY THERMOS WORK?

When I agreed to lend my support to the University Stone Age Society's fundraising drive – to raise money to pay for new spears and broadband internet access – little did I realise that the affair was going to end in ignominy. The idea was that a group of us were to spend a week in a recreation of a Stone Age settlement, deprived of all the comforts of modern living, our privations rewarded with sponsorship income. And while I concede that a Thermos flask is not, strictly speaking, part of Prehistoric Man's primitive toolkit, I strongly refute the accusation that I, in any way, cheated in this challenge.

In particular, I feel that the headline emblazoned across the front page of the college newspaper – "Fraud Flintstone!" – was grossly unwarranted.

Truth to tell, my Thermos is such a constant companion that, when I turned up at the camp, clad in my animal skins and clutching my briefcase, I simply didn't realise I had it with me. After all, it's such an eminently useful apparatus and ever so simple in its design. To understand how it operates, you have to consider the process of heat transfer, or how a liquid alters its temperature to reflect that of its surroundings. This works in three ways: conduction, which usually applies to metals; radiation, which is to do with light; and convection, which is a property of liquid and gases.

Of these three, it is convection that is the important factor in how your Thermos operates. A hot liquid – a bowl of soup, let us say – will heat up the air next to it, which will rise to be replaced by colder air, which in turn will be heated, and so on and so on until soup and air are as hot or as cold as one another. In a Thermos, the liquid, which is housed in a glass receptacle, is separated from the surrounding air by a thin vacuum layer. As a vacuum is defined as a region containing no matter whatsoever, this means that there is no medium through which convection can take place, so the liquid stays as hot or cold as it was when it went into the flask.

Of course, this won't remain the case for ever: heat is gradually lost through the flask's cap and at the point where the inner and outer walls meet. Nevertheless, your trusty Thermos is adequate to meet most needs, such as keeping your soup hot and your ice cubes frozen – and even, I dare say, bringing a little warmth to makeshift Stone Age encampments.

Spoon says...

To remove baked-on grime from pots and baking trays, use a solution of a few teaspoons of bicarbonate of soda in boiling water. This is good for freshening up chopping boards, too.

WHAT IS THE SECRET TO FROTHY CAPPUCCINO?

I seldom holiday overseas. Quite why one should pay a king's ransom to partake of the Mediterranean's questionable diversions when there are perfectly serviceable North Sea resorts such as Cleethorpes, Skegness or Filey is a source of constant bafflement. Take my last holiday abroad, which was spent in Italy. Not only was the food vile (the national cuisine is a curious assemblage of malodorous sausages and frivolously shaped carbohydrates) but I couldn't even get a decent cup of tea at breakfast, the locals instead favouring a scum-topped-coffee affair called 'cappuccino'.

While I wasn't tempted to drink this potation, its surface strata of froth did excite my scientific interest. This is formed by pumping steam through milk, during which process proteins within the milk are adsorbed on to the films surrounding the resultant air bubbles (not absorbed: adsorption is the adhesion of molecules to the surface of solids or liquids with which they are in contact). This gives stability to the bubbles, which collect as froth at the surface. The milk's fat content has an effect upon this foam (skimmed milk, at one per cent fat, creates the greatest volume of froth), as does its temperature (put simply: you'll get more bubbles if your milk is chilled).

Sadly, despite my efforts to stay within Albion's embrace, I am often called abroad through work. Indeed, I'm soon to revisit Italy, to address a convention at Venice's Accademia di Scienza della Cucina. Thankfully, if experience has taught me anything, it is what to pack to help me to endure these foreign jaunts. So while some of the younger delegates might fritter away their free hours in a gondola, I'll be settling down to the detective fiction of Margery Allingham, a tin of arrowroot biscuits and a nice cup of Yorkshire tea. I think we know who has the right idea there, don't we?

Spoon says...

If you are struggling to unscrew the lid of a jar, pierce a small hole in the lid with, say, a corkscrew. This releases the pressure in the jar, so making it much easier to open.

WHY CAN A LARGE LUNCH LEAVE YOU FEELING DROWSY?

To my father, Old Mr Spoon, Sunday lunch was sacrosanct. After a trying working week spent decanting his encyclopaedic knowledge of Greek mythology into the empty vessels of the undergraduate body, he would relish a day of what marketing executives and Americans would, with crushing inevitability, describe as 'me-time'.

Therefore, every Sunday without fail, after Mrs Jeffers had cleared away the remains of the family feast, he would retire to his study to – as he euphemistically put it – "shake hands with Morpheus". Needless to say, it was made abundantly clear to the younger Spoons that during my father's Sunday-afternoon slumbers the study and its environs were strictly out of bounds, any fractious horseplay being banished to the front lawns.

Nevertheless, Old Mr Spoon would, if you asked him, be at pains to point out that these catnaps were not evidence of laziness on his part nor, indeed, a sign that he had drunk too much table wine. This after-lunch torpor arises because, although we get energy from food, we also need to use up a lot of energy to digest it. In fact, the body's energy use can rise by up to 50 per cent during digestion.

To compensate for this, extra blood is sent to the intestine to supply oxygen to fuel the process. So as food enters the stomach, the gut secretes substances that dilate the vessels that supply it with blood. This allows more blood to flow to the digestive tract, which leaves less to go round the rest of the body, with the result that you feel sluggish.

Of course, this is precisely the reason that one should abstain from vigorous exercise following lunch. Physical exertion causes blood to flow away from the gut to the muscles that are being exercised, which can give rise to cramps in the stomach.

Not that this was ever a problem for Old Mr Spoon, you understand. Now I come to think of it, the only Sunday on which I recall him displaying any post-prandial animation was the occasion upon which one of my early experiments on the structural integrity of eggs went so loudly awry. The shout of "Where is that damned boy?!" that rang out from my father's study and the subsequent chase that unfolded through the corridors of Spoon Hall made me wish I had left Mrs Jeffers' new pressure cooker well alone.

Spoon says...

If you are planning to keep broth or stock in the fridge for a few days, don't skim off the fat. This layer of fat will help to keep out germs and other microbes.

PROFESSOR SPOON'S

Obscure spoons

There's so much more to the exciting world of spoons than simply tea, dessert and table...

MONKEY SPOON

Not a utensil used for the consumption of bananas by apes, instead this refers to a ladle used to serve punch. Its name comes from the way it hangs, monkey-like, by its hooked end from the side of the punch bowl.

CADDY SPOON

In the 1700s, tea was pricey. The rich kept theirs under lock in a caddy, and used a caddy spoon to measure tea for the pot. In China, shells were used for this purpose, which is why caddy spoons often have scalloped bowls.

MOUSTACHE SPOON

In the 1870s, moustaches tended towards the huge. This fashion spawned the invention of a special spoon, which had a covered bowl to keep a gentleman's whiskers out of his soup.

RUNCIBLE SPOON

In a case of life imitating art, a runcible spoon, invented by Edward Lear for the owl and the pussy cat to dine on mince and slices of quince with, now describes a three-tined utensil for eating fruit. Sounds like a fork to me...

SNUFF SPOON

Inhaling snuff was a popular pastime in the 17th and 18th centuries. The more genteel snuff-taker would carry a little spoon along with their snuff so they could enjoy the fine-ground tobacco without staining their fingers.

BAFFLING SPOON

Historians of golf will argue that this is not a utensil used for stirring one's tea. They are correct: a baffling spoon is an old golf club, an ancestor of the modern four iron, which I include here only for its delightful name.

DOES OLIVE OIL GO BAD?

Every few months, my sister Valerie and her husband George hire a van to go to Calais, where, in a hangar large enough to fake a Mars landing, they stock up on what they call 'essentials'. In practice, this means that Georgie fills the van with enough cut-price claret to float a battleship, while Val piles her trolley high with the foul sausages, cheeses and pâtés of which our Gallic cousins are so mystifyingly proud. While she's at it, the old girl will also pick up a few gallons of olive oil, but while George's burgundy receives star treatment upon the couple's return, being carefully stowed away in the old boy's cellar, Val's oil is not so fortunate.

Which is a shame, as this is just the kind of treatment it needs to stop it going bad. Olive oil becomes 'rancid' (scientific term) as the result of a process called oxidation, in which oxygen in the air reacts with chemicals in the oil to produce peroxides – compounds that, though possessing the desirable ability to turn a lady's hair yellow, do nothing to enhance the flavours of a Greek salad. This oxidation is accelerated by the oil's contact with air, heat, and light, which means you should always store your oil in a cool, shady place, and not in a clear bottle next to the stove, Valerie.

However, even if you did keep your oil, unopened, in a cellar, it would eventually turn rancid due to auto-oxidation. This process, which occurs in the absence of air, is held in abeyance by the oil's natural antioxidants. Nevertheless, auto-oxidation proceeds, bit by bit, until these antioxidants are all used up, at which point it can quickly become rancid. Sometimes, an old oil (more than three years, say) might taste fine when first exposed to air; however, only a few weeks later, it might taste old and oxidised.

This, though, is not the calamity you might suppose. As I said to my sister on the latest occasion on which her French consignment spoiled, many of the world's people routinely eat rancid oil (usually due to historical and cultural factors and a lack of proper storage conditions) and some even prefer its taste. As for myself, I added, I was no great disciple of olive oil, rancid or otherwise, being more of a lard man.

Sadly, my observations provided curiously scant consolation for the old girl, although I fail to see quite how Valerie's intemperate suggestion as to what I might do with my lard would help matters.

Spoon says...

Aubergines absorb lots of oil when they are fried. But if you salt them first (for 30 minutes or so), rinse them, then squeeze them dry, they will absorb less.

WHY DO MY YORKSHIRE PUDDINGS COLLAPSE?

Even to this day, the waft of baking Yorkshire puddings makes me think of postage stamps. You see, philately was one of a series of pastimes with which my father attempted to fire my youthful enthusiasm. Old Mr Spoon reasoned that if I could be encouraged to see the appeal of a British Guiana Penny Magenta, then I'd be less likely to devote myself to the pursuit of science – with the happy consequence that I'd also be less likely blow up the staff quarters with my experiments.

Sadly for my father, I was lost to philately the moment I started to think about the adhesive gum on the reverse of my new stamps. This substance, I soon found, is a polysaccharide called dextrin, which was first identified back in 1804 by the heroically named French chemist, Edme Jean-Baptiste Bouillon-LaGrange His discovery – which, doubtless to the Frenchman's mystification, attained the nickname British gum – was used for fixing dyes, making inks and, in solution, as the sticky stuff on the back of stamps.

Dextrin is also, if I may guide you back to the subject under discussion, the substance that causes Yorkshire puddings to remain rigid. When the starches in the pudding batter are exposed to heat, they undergo a process of dextrinisation. In scientific terms, this simply means that they've been converted into dextrin; in lay terms, it means they've gone crispy. Either way, the upshot is that your Yorkshires will now support their own weight.

After my discovery of Bouillon-LaGrange, I returned with renewed vigour to my scientific researches and, once again, the staff quarters resounded to the explosive report of my experimentation. All this, alas, was too much for my long-suffering father who, despite all his efforts, was forced to concede ruefully that philately had got him precisely nowhere.

Spoon says…

A few rice grains in your salt or sugar stops either getting damp because the rice absorbs any moisture in the air. Just make sure you don't put it in your tea or sprinkle it on your chips!

DOES TINNED FOOD STAY FRESH FOREVER?

There is a short answer to this science fiction-style question, although, generous soul that I am, I will indulge you a while. As 'forever' is, semantically speaking, an infinite concept, the idea that the tin of pineapple chunks you bought in 1977 – and which has languished at the back of your pantry ever since – will still be as its maker intended long after the human drama has reached its final act is, frankly, ludicrous.

The process of canning was invented in 1795 by a Frenchman, Nicholas Appert, who was seeking a way to keep fresh the provisions of Napoleon's troops. Appert found he could extend a food's edible life by heating it, then sealing it in an airtight container (he used glass jars; the first metal tins were used in 1810 to provision the British soldiers who would face Napoleon at Waterloo five years later). It works because, during canning, food is heated to such a degree that the micro-organisms which cause it to go off are killed. It's then sealed to protect it from airborne microbes.

However, any food will react with the tin in which it's housed, causing taste and texture changes that lower its nutritional value. Forces of chaos are at work from outside the tin, too. Over time, the tin's metal will oxidise. When this rust is deep enough, tiny holes will open up in the tin's surface which, once again, render the food within vulnerable to micro-organisms.

So while it may be tempting to imagine a race of moon-dwelling future humans supplementing their one-pill diets with the odd can of 21st-century spaghetti hoops, it is, nonetheless, a ridiculous image, which should be resisted by all except children, the simple minded and those for whom the unfettering of the imagination is professionally advantageous. Writers of science fiction, for instance. The short answer, by the way, was 'no'.

Spoon says...

Avoid tears when chopping onions by chilling them beforehand. Refrigeration minimises the release of the volatile sulphide gas, allicin, which is the cause of the eyes' irritation.

DOES WHITE WINE REMOVE RED-WINE STAINS?

Like many of her proud race, Mrs Jeffers, our Scottish housekeeper at Spoon Hall, was wilfully partial to the produce of her homeland. In particular, she was a staunch advocate of Irn Bru, which, as well as drinking by the crate load, she would turn to a host of household uses. She'd use it to remove rust stains, to return the sheen to my father's polo trophies, and most curiously of all, to lift red-wine stains from fabric.

Sadly (and perhaps unsurprisingly), her deployment of lurid carbonated beverages upon hard-to shift household stains seldom, if ever, produced the desired result. This was rather unfortunate for my father, who was as fond of a drop of claret as he was clumsy, and whose treasured polar-bearskin rug – a fixture of his study – soon began to look as if it had been fabricated from the collected pelts of tortoiseshell cats. Nevertheless, Mrs J wouldn't have been any better served by pouring white wine on such spillages. Other things that won't shift red wine include soda water, cream of tartar and salt – which is actually used to fix colour in the dyeing industry.

The chemistry of colour is hugely complex, but, in short, red wine gets its colour from compounds called anthocyanidins. The molecules of these pigments are held together by a series of strong double bonds, and it is these that must be destroyed for the stain to vanish. This is best done with an oxidising agent, which will degrade the pigment to smaller, colourless molecules. One option is to use a weak hydrogen peroxide solution, but take care: hydrogen peroxide will attack all the pigments in your fabric, not just those you want to remove, so test it on a tiny corner of material first.

By far the better option, as Old Mrs J herself might have counselled in her more lucid moments, is not to spill your wine in the first place.

Spoon says...

Store eggs in the body of your fridge, rather than on special fridge-door shelves. This way, they are exposed to fewer temperature fluctuations, and will stay fresher for longer.

WHY DOES
LIMESCALE
FORM IN MY
KETTLE?

My young research assistant, Edie, is a most respectful and attentive student. Indeed, many is the time I've looked up from my work to see her pale blue eyes turned towards me in a rapt attitude of what I can only suppose to be academic admiration. She is also a helpful girl, often bringing me in cakes, doing my filing and making tea, although her record in this latter field is rather chequered. Only this week, for instance, I had to upbraid her when the final mouthful of my mid-morning cuppa left me spitting shards of limescale across the lab.

I must admit that I was rather taken aback at how crestfallen Edie looked at this turn of events. Nevertheless, as I pointed out to her at the time, a good chemist should know that in a hard-water area such as ours, one needs to be keep a constant watch against the build up of limescale. By 'hard water', I should say, I don't mean ice, as some of the more featherbrained members of my undergraduate class are apt to believe. No, hard-water areas are those where a higher proportion of the supply is drawn from natural (as opposed to man-made) reservoirs, to which the water has had to flow over and seep through rock to reach, dissolving minerals such as calcium and magnesium as it does so.

When this water is heated, as in a kettle or a hot-water pipe, the dissolved mineral calcium hydrogencarbonate is converted into calcium carbonate. This is insoluble in water and so is left behind as solid limescale. Or "$Ca(HCO_3)_2 \rightarrow CaCO_3 + CO_2 + H_2O$", as the new notice I have affixed next to the kettle in our faculty kitchen helpfully displays.

Happily, by the end of the day Edie was back to her usual chipper self, even volunteering to stay behind to help with that evening's experiments. When I suggested that surely she had a young man she should be getting off home to, she replied very decidedly that none of the chaps of her own age possessed the "professorial gravitas" that she was seeking.

"You had better be careful, Edie," I joked, "or you'll end up with an old buffer like me."

I'm pleased to report that my respectful young assistant had the good grace not to look as appalled by this nightmarish vision of her potential future as she must surely have felt…

Spoon says…

Collect vegetable offcuts, tomato seeds, onion skins, and meat and chicken scraps in plastic bags and store them in your freezer. When you have enough, make stock.

INDEX